Very Rare
GLASSWARE
of the Depression Years
Second Series

Gene Florence

COLLECTOR BOOKS
A Division of Schroeder Publishing Co., Inc.

Other books by Gene Florence

Elegant Glassware of the Depression Era, Revised 4th Edition $19.95
Kitchen Glassware of the Depression Years, 4th Edition $19.95
Pocket Guide to Depression Glass, 7th Edition ....$ 9.95
Collector's Encyclopedia of Depression Glass, 9th Edition $19.95
Collector's Encyclopedia of Occupied Japan I..$14.95
Collector's Encyclopedia of Occupied Japan II...$14.95
Collector's Encyclopedia of Occupied Japan III $14.95
Collector's Encyclopedia of Occupied Japan IV $14.95
Very Rare Glassware of the Depression Years..$24.95
Very Rare Glassware of the Depression Years, 2nd Series............................$24.95
Gene Florence's Standard Baseball Guide Price Guide, 3rd Edition..............$ 9.95

Additional copies of this book may be ordered from:

COLLECTOR BOOKS
P.O. Box 3009
Paducah, Kentucky 42002-3009
or
Gene Florence
P.O. Box 22186
Lexington, Kentucky 40522

@$24.95 Add $2.00 for postage and handling.

Copyright: Gene Florence, 1991

This book or any part thereof may not be reproduced without the written consent of the Author and Publisher.

Table of Contents

Foreword

The acceptance of the first *Very Rare Glassware of the Depression Years* was overwhelming. I had little idea how collectors would respond to a "picture" book of rarely found items. That first book has already been reprinted twice and one of the limited (500) leather bound copies recently sold for a premuim price! As an author who loves his work, I can only thank you, my readers for the confidence that you have placed in my work.

Actually, this second book was easier to do than the first in many ways. Establishing a successful format is the most difficult part of any price guide; and since that was already done, all I had to do was simply find enough rare items for another book! I am only showing rare pieces that encompass the time period and patterns shown in my other Depression era books.

Finding the glassware was somewhat easier this time since many collectors sought me out to advise me of their treasures after seeing the first book. Without you keeping a watch for unknown glassware pieces, I could never have found enough pieces to put this book together as quickly as I was able.

Photographs for this book were taken over a three-year period, whereas the first book was mostly photographed during a week-long session. As newly discovered items or unusual colors of commonly found pieces were discovered, I had them photographed at the earliest opportunity. This sounds simple enough, but when you are dealing with a commercial photographer with thousands of prints and a publisher with hundreds of books in the works, photographs sometime end up missing! It is difficult to get some pieces to show both color and pattern; but finally getting it photographed, even if it took two or three photography sessions to do it, never seemed to solve the problem of where the print was when you needed it!

Rare glass keeps being found! I have already photographed seven pieces for a possible third book. Only yesterday, in Ohio, I found a creamer and sugar in a major Depression glass pattern in a color I did not know existed! Keep looking; maybe you will find some of the items shown in this or the first book. Unbelievably, so many readers found the heretofore elusive Heisey Crystolite cake stand after it was shown in the first book that it is no longer considered rare! It is still avidly sought, however. Glass enthusiasts hope that will happen to some of the items shown in this book!

Hopefully, you will appreciate our efforts in putting this second book on rare Depression era glassware together. I hope it helps you find some *rare* glass!

Acknowledgments

Many collectors have loaned their rare glass for photographs in this book, and each is acknowledged with the items shown. However, many collectors went beyond lending glass to be shown. A special thanks to Beverly Hines and her friend, Arline Moffett, who traveled from Cajun country to bring glassware to be photographed. Dick and Pat Spencer brought not only their glass, but the glass of a dozen other collectors from Illinois and Missouri. Lottie Porter and Vivian McMahon came from Michigan with Lottie's glass. All of these fine folks helped unpack and repack their prized glassware for photography so that you could see the rarest Depression era glassware that can be found. If it were not for these special people who are willing to share their collections with others, a book of this magnitude would be nearly impossible.

Lynn Welker and the Cambridge Glass Club Museum have allowed me to borrow some of their rarities in order for you to see some of the beautiful glassware made by Cambridge. The Cambridge Club members have made their acquisitions accessible to me in order to promote collecting of Cambridge glassware. Be sure to see the Club Museum if you are ever in Cambridge, Ohio!

Photography for this book was done by Tom Clouser of Curtis and Mays Studio in Paducah, Kentucky. The photograph for the American Sweetheart lamp was furnished by Jim and Dot Kimball of California.

Family has always been a great help to me in my work. Mom, "Grannie Bear," lists and packs glass for all the photography sessions with my sons, Chad and Marc helping my Dad load unload glass for each session. That broken wrist really slowed me down in that department for a while. Cathy, my wife, continues to be my proofreader and general taskmaster. She tries to put my varied ideas in a readable form for the public. She and her mother do most of the packing and collating of patterns of glass for the photography sessions. No one likes the way I pack!

Many people work behind the scenes to put a book together. Much praise belongs to unseen workers who make this book a viable product. Layout is vital. It is important to get picture and type sizes to fit and all horizontal photos and verticals to blend; and placing patterns alphabetical by company does create a layout problem or two! Jane White of Collector Books is responsible for the meshing of this into a workable format. Besides Cathy, Grannie Bear and me, proofing and correcting were done by Lisa Stroup and Beth Ray. All the headaches and other problems with photographs disappearing and deadlines being met were dumped on editor, Steve Quertermous. If I've overlooked someone, forgive me. It was unintentional. Please know I'm grateful for all your efforts. I could not have done this book without you!

AKRO AGATE COMPANY 1911-1951

Akro Agate Company was originally established in Akron, Ohio, in 1911. It made marbles and games there until the company moved to Clarksburg, West Virginia, in October of 1914 for economic reasons. Clarksburg offered a good grade of sand and cheap natural gas. These were the two most needed materials for making glass marbles.

World War I helped to establish Akro Agate Company as a major force in the making of marbles. Up until that war, the importing of marbles from Germany had kept Akro Agate a fledgling business. With the demise of European competition due to the war, Akro Agate was able to entrench itself in the field of marble making to the point that by the Depression years, they manufactured 75% of the marbles made in the United States.

A competitor, Master Marbles, cut into Akro's business when it hired some of the machine designers working at Akro. For today's collectors, that was a fortuitous turning point. Because of losing business in the marble industry, Akro then turned to making other objects out of the same materials. Flower pots, planters and other utility items made by Akro grew out of the failing marble production. After obtaining the moulds from Westite Glass Company in 1936, when that factory burned, Akro issued a strong line of these items that prospered until World War II. During the last half of the 1930's, they made a line of children's doll dishes, tobacco accessory items (ashtrays, match holders, etc.) and other utilitarian lines using the same glass material as had been used in their marbles. The doll or "play" dishes became a major line when "metal" play dishes disappeared due to the metals being needed for war materials. As Akro Agate had prospered during WWI, it again prospered because of WWII.

Ironically, the fate of this little company was sealed at the end of the war, however, with the introduction of plastic doll dishes which were increasingly available from Japan. In 1951, Akro was sold to Clarksburg Glass Company; and today, collectors search for that elusive trademark (crow flying through the letter A). The Akro was a shortened form of this — "as a crow."

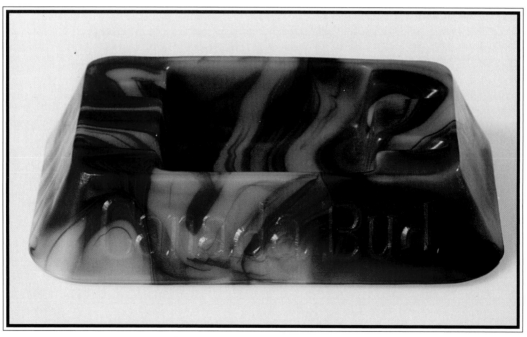

CANADA BUD ashtray - rare advertising item

This Akro mould shape is unusual, but it is the advertising of this Canadian beer that makes it so collectible. Advertising items are eagerly sought, but a story goes with this one. According to a knowledgeable collector of advertising brewery memorabilia, Anheuser-Busch sued and got the name of this beer changed before many advertisements for it were made. This makes for some interesting competition in buying the three known specimens.

CAMBRIDGE GLASS COMPANY 1902-1958

The Cambridge Glass Company was started in Cambridge, Ohio, in 1902. Glass was made there until 1958 except for a short period in 1954-1955 when the plant was closed. Today, there is a National Cambridge Collector's Club. Many of the pieces shown in this section were borrowed from the Cambridge Museum which is operated by that club and located on Rt. 40E in Cambridge, Ohio.

The glass photographed in this section represents patterns made during a time period (1930's to 1950's) that are most collected today. Collectors of Cambridge glass began collecting the glass by colors and decorations that were distinctly Cambridge. However, as more and more Depression glass collectors started to notice the finer handmade glassware from Cambridge, dinnerware lines and sets began to be gathered. Thus, a new standard of collecting was created and the prices started rising.

All of the glass shown in this section which was lent by Lynn Welker can be viewed at the Cambridge Museum.

If you are interested in joining the National Cam-bridge Collectors Club, their address is: National Cambridge Collectors, Inc., P.O. Box 416GF, Cambridge, Ohio 43725. Dues are $15.00 a year.

The following pages show some of the rarest pieces of Cambridge known in the dinnerware lines with emphasis on color rarities as well as unusual pieces.

From the collection of Lynn Welker

APPLE BLOSSOM Gold Krystol #3400 puff box and perfume with original tray - rare item

APPLE BLOSSOM
#3400 pitcher - rare color
Heatherbloom

From the collection of Bill and Barbara Adt

APPLE BLOSSOM
dark Emerald Green pitcher -
rare color

Author's Collection

APPLE BLOSSOM amethyst #3400 pitcher and tumbler - rare color

From the collection of Cliff and Lydia McNeil

APPLE BLOSSOM Statuesque #3011/2 table goblet - rare item

APPLE BLOSSOM amber #3400/46 cabinet flask - rare color

CAPRICE amethyst Daulton-style 90 oz. pitcher in Faberware holder

CAPRICE crystal pressed water goblet, unknown stemware line (400?) - rare item

CHANTILLY Ebony, gold-encrusted 11" vase #278 - rare color

CHANTILLY
#3400/92 ball-shaped
32 oz. decanter

Author's Collection

CHANTILLY
crystal, 4¾" tall,
28 oz. pitcher - unusual style

Author's Collection

CHANTILLY crystal quarter-pound butter dish - rare item

CLEO Peach-Blo #747, 3" candlestick - rarely etched

CLEO Royal Blue Decagon 11" center-handled sandwich tray - rare color

CLEO Peach-Blo sugar sifter, tall ewer and tray - tray rarely etched

CLEO Peach-Blo #1070, 36 oz. pinch decanter - rarely found etched

CLEO Peach-Blo 9" toast and cover - rare item
This looks more like a cheese dish than a toast, but it has holes in the lid to allow steam to escape.

CLEO Willow Blue footed water tumbler (unknown blank) - rare item

DIANE Carmen, gold-encrusted #3122 goblet - rare color

DIANE crystal #7801 hollow stem champagne - rare item

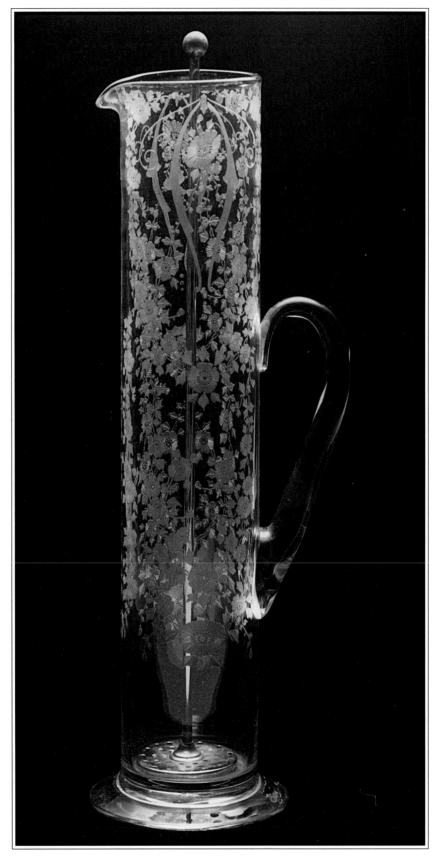

DIANE crystal 60 oz. cocktail churn (martini pitcher) - rare item

DIANE crystal cornucopia vase - rare item

From the collection of Cliff and Lydia McNeil

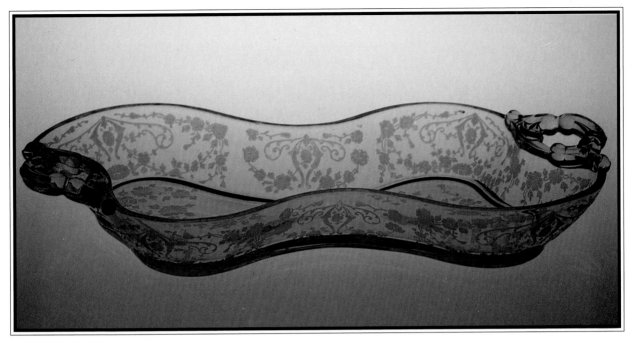

DIANE light Emerald Green #3400 two-handled relish - rare color

From the collection of Cliff and Lydia McNeil

DIANE
Peach-Blo #3400/92
ball-shaped 32 oz. decanter -
rare color

DIANE Crown Tuscan, gold-encrusted #3011 (Statuesque) cigarette box
and cover - rare item and color

DIANE Crown Tuscan, gold-encrusted #3011 (Statuesque) ashtray

ELAINE "Whimsy" made from candy or urn bottom - rare item

Many times items made by workers and taken home years ago have become collectors items today.

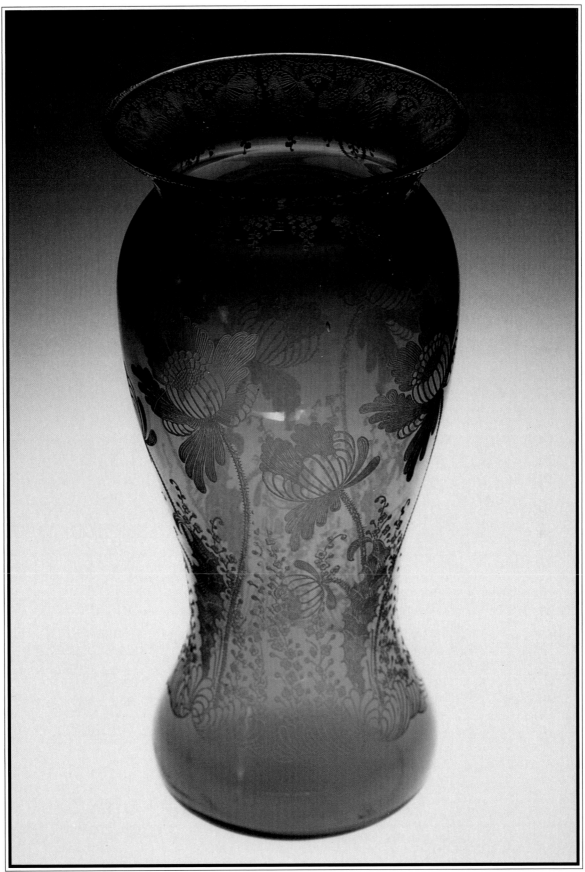

GLORIA dark Emerald Green 12" vase #1335 - rare color and item

GLORIA dark Emerald Green #1323, 28 oz. decanter and shot glass - rare color

When we first photographed these, they were pictured individually. I looked through catalogues for several hours trying to find out what the strange-shaped vase was before I realized the photo was a close-up of a shot glass.

GLORIA amber #3400/141, 80 oz. pitcher - rare color

GLORIA Royal Blue, gold-encrusted #3400, 12" vase - rare color

HUNT SCENE amber, gold-encrusted #525 cocktail shaker - rare item

Cambridge Glass Company

HUNT SCENE
light Emerald Green
#3077, 1 oz. cordial - rare item

HUNT SCENE
light Emerald Green
#3075, 2 oz. shot glass - rare item

34

HUNT SCENE #1025, 6" Ebony gold-encrusted cigar humidor - rare item

This humidor was purchased in Seattle at the Green River Depression Glass show in February 1990. I had received an excellent photograph of another one from a collector in Texas, but I was able to find one myself in time for this book.

MT. VERNON #102 green opalescent individual salt - experimental color

MT. VERNON
Azurite #2795, 3" round
toilet box - rare color

From the collection of Lynn Welker

MT. VERNON
Carmen cologne bottle - rare color

From the collection of Lynn Welker

PORTIA
Carmen, gold-encrusted #1066 oval
cigarette or card holder - rare color

ROSALIE (#731) Bluebell 6 oz. sherbet - rare color

This color has not been found on any other etched dinnerware lines that are shown in my books.

Author's Collection

Right:
ROSALIE
light Emerald Green Gyro Optic
10" vase - rare item

Below:
ROSALIE (#731) and APPLE BLOSSOM
light Emerald Green #893, 12" handled
serving tray - rare item

Very unusual in that this piece contains Rosalie
in the middle, but is etched Apple Blossom
around the outside edge.

Author's Collection

ROSALIE (#731)
Topaz bowl with Willow Blue stem #3115, 9 oz. goblet - rare color combination

ROSALIE (#731) Peach-Blo #755 Decagon 14" bowl - rare item

ROSEPOINT Amber #279 13" footed vase - rare color

ROSEPOINT crystal #3104, 3½ oz. cocktail - rare item

ROSEPOINT crystal #1380, 26 oz. square decanter - rare item

Author's Collection

Right:
ROSEPOINT Carmen, gold-encrusted #3500
1 oz. cordial - rare item

Below:
ROSEPOINT crystal #3400/69 after dinner
cup and saucer - rare item

From the collection of Lynn Welker

ROSEPOINT crystal pressed Rosepoint water goblet with etched
Rosepoint bowl - rare item

This goblet vividly illustrates the difference in "pressed" and
"etched" Rosepoint pieces. The pressed Rosepoint pattern is
moulded onto the base, whereas the acid etched pattern was
added to the bowl. It is rare because *both* styles are on one item.

From the collection of Cliff and Lydia McNeil

VALENCIA Peach-Blo #3500/16, 11" footed console bowl - rare color

The bowl and the candlestick shown next are the only known pieces of Valencia in color.

VALENCIA Peach-Blo #3500/31, 6" candlestick - rare color

WILDFLOWER Topaz #1299, 11" footed vase - rare color

Cambridge Glass Company

WILDFLOWER Emerald, gold-encrusted #1238, 12" vase - rare color

WILDFLOWER crystal #3116 cut water goblet - rare item

The pattern has been cut into this goblet instead of the usual acid etching of the pattern.

FEDERAL GLASS COMPANY 1900-1984

Federal Glass Company was founded in Columbus, Ohio and really prospered during the Depression with its dinnerware sets in pink, blue, green and the prolific use of amber known as "Golden Glo" in the patterns of Madrid, Patrician, Sharon and Parrot.

Federal became the first major company to reproduce a pattern from the Depression era with each piece marked. This "Recollection" pattern was the original Madrid, issued in 1976 for the Bicentennial and marked with '76 on each piece.

MADRID "Golden Glo" lazy susan - rare item

Seven hot plates (cold plates?) rest atop the walnut turntable. There is a decal on the bottom of this that says "Kalter Aufschain Cold Cuts Server Schrimer Cincy." Even though these coasters have always been called "hot" maybe they should have been called "cold." The middle coaster shows the difference between the plain coasters and the indented ones. It is the *wooden part* that is rare!

PARROT "Golden Glo" butter dish - rare color

There have only been three complete *amber* butters found, although green ones turn up frequently.

PARROT Springtime green 5" round
hot plate - rare item

Only two of the round hot plates have been found, but there have been over a dozen of the Parrot hot plates found with the pointed edges like those found in Madrid. (See page 52.)

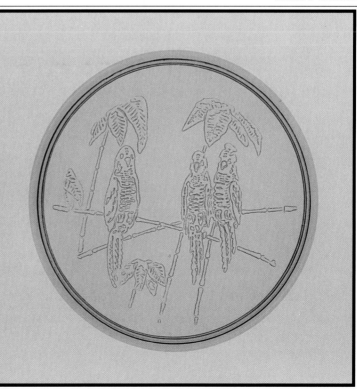

FOSTORIA GLASS COMPANY 1887-1986

Fostoria Glass Company almost survived a century! That included a major move from Fostoria, Ohio to Moundsville, West Virginia, in the early days. Lancaster Colony bought Fostoria in the early 1980's but even the glassware in the morgue at the factory was sold in December 1986.

The American pattern, first begun in 1915, was one of the longest made patterns in the U.S. glassmaking history! Lancaster Colony is continuing to make pieces available in this pattern through Indiana Glass Company and Dalzell Viking Glass Company.

AMERICAN Amethyst 12 oz. beer mug - rare color

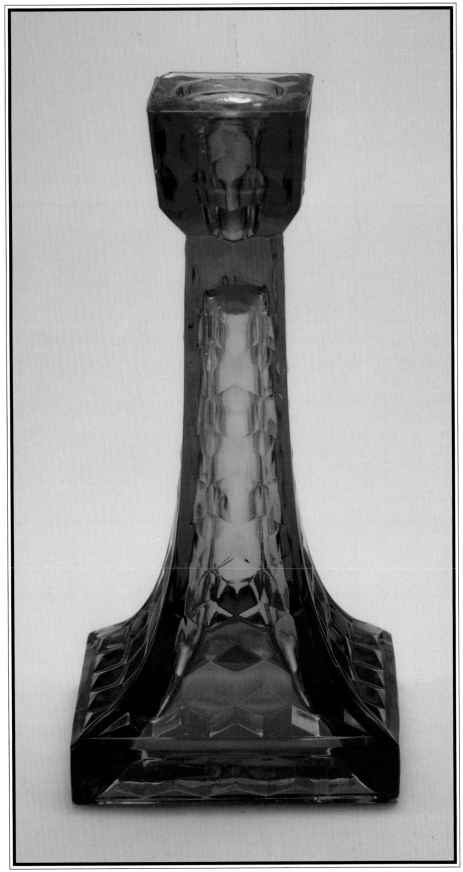

AMERICAN blue 7¼" candlestick - rare color

AMERICAN blue Tom & Jerry punch bowl - rare color and style

Another bowl in green has been found like this blue one. So far these are the only known ones in this shape. Finally, one of these punch bowls has been found in crystal.

AMERICAN crystal swung vase - rare item

This 12" vase was swung from either an old style pitcher without handles or a porch vase.

AMERICAN crystal soap dish - rare item

There are three ledges inside the bowl for the insert to rest upon.

CHINTZ
red lamp with gold-decorated pattern -
rare color and item

COLONY green 11" vase - rare color and piece

No sooner had I shown a crystal vase like this in the first rare book than this green one also appeared. This is actually Queen Anne which later became Fostoria's Colony.

JUNE blue 6" blown comport - rare item

JUNE yellow soup bowl - rare item

NAVARRE crystal 16 oz. carafe - rare item

NAVARRE green dinner bell - rare color

TROJAN Topaz #2439 decanter - rare item

VERSAILLES blue #2439 decanter - rare item

VESPER amber Mah Jongg set - rare item

VESPER amber butter dish - rare item

This is the only known example of an amber Vesper butter.

HAZEL-ATLAS GLASS COMPANY 1902-1956

Hazel-Atlas was formed from the merger of Hazel Glass Company and Atlas Glass and Metal Company in 1902. Production of containers and tumblers were their main concern until the Depression years. In the 1930's, starting with kitchenware items such as colored mixing bowls, they quickly branched into dinnerware patterns.

The Shirley Temple bowl, mug and creamer that are recognized by almost everyone were made by Hazel Atlas. Sets of Royal Lace and Moderntone in Ritz blue (cobalt) were advertised together for the same price: 44 pieces for $2.99! Now, there is a much greater price range in those patterns!

In recent years, it has been the kitchenware made by Hazel-Atlas that has come to the forefront. Again, the popularity of Ritz blue has pushed the prices of that color well above the prices for pink and green. Mixing bowls, measuring cups and reamers all command premium prices. The piece may be rarer in some other color, but collector demand pushes the price of the blue well beyond those of any other color.

COLONIAL BLOCK Ritz blue creamer - rare color

FLORENTINE NO. 2 crystal decorated vase - unique item

Many times these uncut tumblers were designed to be vases. This shows what a glass worker sometimes did in his leisure time.

FLORENTINE NO. 2 pink sherbet on Madrid shaped mould - rare item

Madrid was made by Federal and not Hazel-Atlas which makes this an interesting story as is also the case of the tumbler below which is on a Jeannette mould blank.

FLORENTINE NO. 2 pink lemonade tumbler on Floral blank - rare item

I originally bought this tumbler in the early 1970's at the Washington Court House, Ohio, flea market for $1.00 and after photographing it for an early book, gave it to a dealer in Beverly, Kansas, to sell to a collector of pink Florentine in Louisiana. I never did get the $25.00 for it because the dealer "forgot" it. This tumbler was bought from another dealer in Denver at a Depression Glass show. He explained that he had bought the tumbler from the dealer in Kansas after I asked him from whom he had purchased it. I ended up buying it again for considerably more than my original purchase price.

From the collection of Bill and Lottie Porter

FLORENTINE NO. 2
fired-on orange cup and
saucer - unusual item

From the collection of Bill and Lottie Porter

FLORENTINE NO. 2
fired-on blue cup and
saucer - unusual item

FRUITS green rolled edge bowl made from 8" plate - unique item

Author's Collection

Author's Collection

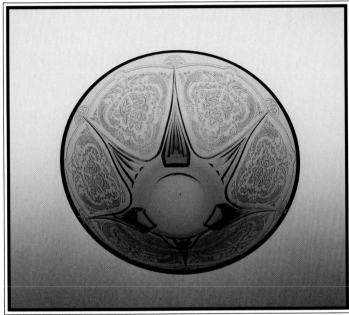

ROYAL LACE green, cobalt blue and pink
nut bowls - rare items

The nut bowls are straight-sided candle holders without the holder in the center. The cobalt
blue has been turned on its side so you can
see the inside better.

Author's Collection

A.H. HEISEY & COMPANY 1896-1957

The A.H. Heisey & Company opened its door in 1896. Their handsome pressed glassware was a success. In fact, the innovative idea of advertising glassware in national publications is attributed to Heisey. Glass was made continuously at the plant site in Newark, Ohio, until 1957. As with Cambridge, the glassware made in the 1930's to 1950's is the most collectible today.

One of the most difficult problems facing new collectors comes from the fact that the Heisey moulds were bought by Imperial in 1958, and many pieces were made at that plant until its demise in 1984. New collectors have to learn the Imperial colors because some of these pieces made by Imperial are similar to rare Heisey colors. Crystal pieces are more difficult to distinguish and collectors are beginning to accept this fact. Almost all of those Heisey/Imperial moulds were repurchased by the Heisey Collectors of America, Inc. and are now back in Newark, Ohio. So, there should be no danger of reissues being made from these moulds again.

From the collection of Charles and Cecelia Larsen

LARIAT amber high sherbet - rare color

LODESTAR Dawn candlestick - rare color and item

OCTAGON Hawthorne with Moongleam handles creamer and sugar - rare color

ORCHID crystal Waverly lemon dish - rare item
(shown from both sides)

ORCHID crystal 14" vase - rare item

PLANTATION crystal cigarette box - rare item

PLANTATION crystal 5" epergne candle holder - rare item

PROVENCIAL zircon vase - rare item and color

SATURN zircon candlestick 2-lite - rare item and color

From the collection of Charles and Cecelia Larsen

COBALT BLUE Old Williamsburg pilsner - rare color and item

TANGERINE Empress cup
and saucer - rare color

TANGERINE Empress creamer - rare color

TANGERINE Empress sugar - rare color

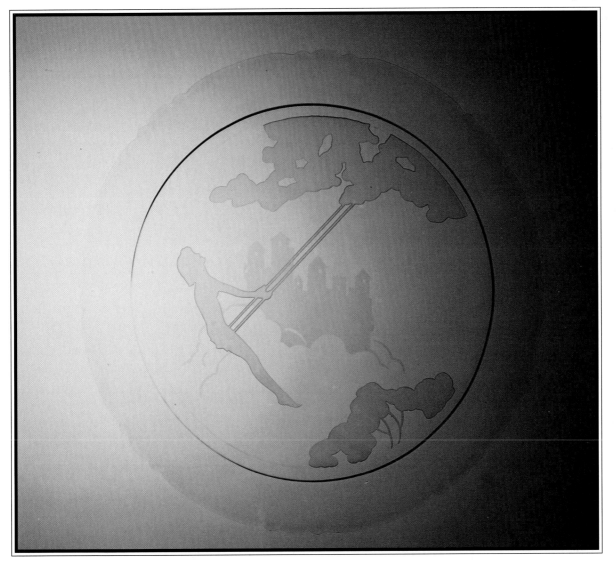

EMPRESS crystal plate, Maxfield Parrish - rare item

HOCKING GLASS COMPANY 1905 to Date

Hocking became today's Anchor-Hocking in 1937, but nearly all of the glassware shown in this section was made before the year of that merger. The people who work at this factory have always helped me in every way they could in my research because they realize the historical significance of our glass. I am truly grateful.

Author's Collection

CAMEO crystal shaker - rare color

I have owned seven pink Cameo shakers, but this is the only crystal one I have ever heard of in any collection.

CAMEO green 3½" wine goblet - rare item

The rare one is pictured on the left beside the regular 4" wine for comparison.

FIRE-KING DINNERWARE "PHILBE" blue 7¼", 9 oz. water goblet -
rare item

FIRE-KING DINNERWARE "PHILBE" blue 4" candy jar - rare color

This, the only known blue candy, first surfaced in Michigan in 1976 and has been in a collection in Florida until early 1990. It now is in a Texas collector's hands.

FIRE-KING DINNERWARE "PHILBE" green cookie jar - rare item

I originally purchased this cookie jar at the Washington Court House, Ohio, flea market in the early 1970's for $10.00 and later sold it to a "collector" friend for $10.00. She (collector?) sold it a few months later to a collector of cookie jars for $300.00. It stayed in California for years, but was sold and I finally bought it back in early 1990 for a considerably greater sum than originally purchased. It now resides in another collection in Oregon.

MAYFAIR green 60 oz. pitcher - rare color

Note the fuller pattern on this pitcher than is normally found on a Mayfair pitcher. This collector owns two 60 oz. pitchers in green and their patterns and shades of green are considerably different.

MAYFAIR pink 4⅛", 2½ oz. cocktail - rare item

The regular cocktail is pictured on the left for comparison. Note that the rare one has a thinner stem and has a more cone-shaped bowl. Only five of these have ever been found so look closely for the difference.

MAYFAIR pink vase - rare item

Originally bought in Michigan at a flea market for 50¢ in the mid-1970's. It took me eight years to finally purchase this after I originally saw it. It is now in the same collection as the footed shaker.

MAYFAIR pink miniature berry bowl - rare item

MAYFAIR yellow 9" octagonal bowl - rare item

MISS AMERICA Jade-ite salad plate - rare color

Very few pieces of Miss America have ever been found in this color.

PRINCESS green footed pitcher and tumbler - rare items

HOCKING
blue 40 oz. canister - rare color

HOCKING blue batter bowl - rare color

IMPERIAL GLASS CORPORATION 1904-1984

Although glass making began at Imperial in 1904, it was the start of a new era in 1936 when Candlewick was introduced for the first time. Until the company's demise in 1984, Imperial turned out a multitude of pieces in this one pattern, but it was not their ONLY pattern.

BEADED BLOCK pink pitcher - rare color

This is the only *pink* pitcher I have seen, but I have now seen three in white.

CANDLEWICK crystal "whimsy" bowl made from old style basket without a handle - rare item

This piece astounded me at the 1990 Houston show. The bowl sold during set-up for $195.00 to a dealer who put it in his booth for $350.00. About an hour later, it was purchased by another dealer for $300.00, and as he was walking back to his booth (which was beside mine), another dealer purchased it from him for $500.00. The last dealer made more than the bowl originally sold for! At last contact, the bowl was priced at $750.00!

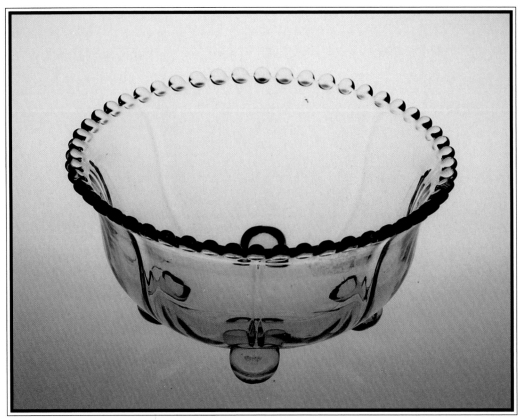

CANDLEWICK blue #400/74J lily bowl - rare color

CANDLEWICK frosted crystal oval lamp shade with Cut 800 - rare item

Several of these were found in original marked boxes.

CANDLEWICK crystal #400/225 goblet - rare item

From the collection of Ronnie Marshall Vickers

CANDLEWICK crystal #440/15 4" tumbler - rare item

CANDLEWICK crystal #400/680 twin hurricane lamp - rare item

It takes five pieces to complete this with two adapters and two hurricane shades.

CANDLEWICK crystal #400/26 hurricane lamp - rare item

Adapters to hold the shades for the hurricane on page 103 and this one are not interchangeable!

CANDLEWICK crystal #400/75N lily bowl - rare item

Only made in 1939 so there are not many of these found in collections.

CANDLEWICK crystal candle with hurricane shade with red bird
and floral decoration #400/79 - rare decoration

CANDLEWICK
crystal 4" Boudoir clocks - rare items

Note the two different styles of edge beading which I have never reported before.

CANDLEWICK crystal #400/187 7" footed bud vase - rare item

CANDLEWICK green tidbit set - rare color

CANDLEWICK red footed, 15 oz. handled cordial decanter -
rare color

CANDLEWICK red #400/52D 7½" two-handled plate - rare color

CANDLEWICK
red #400/52C 6¾" two-handled
crimped plate - rare color

INDIANA GLASS COMPANY 1907 to Date

Indiana Glass has caused concern for collectors for years with their "re-issues." A more proper term might be reproductions! It is a shame because many pieces of their glass fit the "rare" category.

NO. 610, "PYRAMID" crystal 11 oz. footed tumbler - rare item

From the collection of Clarence Clark

TEA ROOM pink 11" ruffled edge vase - rare item

JEANNETTE GLASS COMPANY

Jeannette Glass Company seemed to have an affinity for making odd-colored glass from their standard glassware lines. Canary yellow (vaseline), red or even Delphite blue turns up in patterns once in a while. To make this fact even more astounding is that those colors were not part of their repertoire in other patterns either. It's as if they wanted to cause us wonderment years later.

From the collection of Dan Tucker and Lorrie Kitchen

ADAM
Delphite blue candlestick - rare color

You have to turn over the candlestick in order to see the pattern, so I have given you both views.

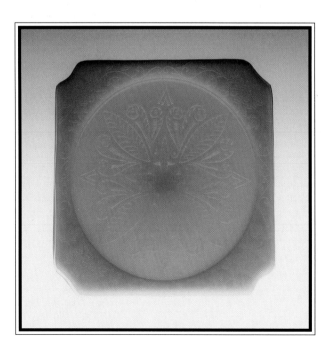

CHERRY BLOSSOM pink cookie jar - rare item

Originally bought for $1.00 at a flea market in Pennsylvania. The lid was taped on and it was tossed over the back of a pick-up truck to the buyer!

CHERRY BLOSSOM orange slag three-footed bowl - rare color

Two views are shown to see the pattern and the color.

From the collection of George and Veronica Sionakides

DORIC AND PANSY Ultramarine 4¼", 10 oz. tumbler -
rare item

SUNFLOWER Delphite blue cup and saucer - rare color

WINDSOR blue butter dish - rare color

From the collection of George and Veronica Sionakides

WINDSOR pink tab-handled berry bowl - rare item

From the collection of Kevin and Barbara Kiley

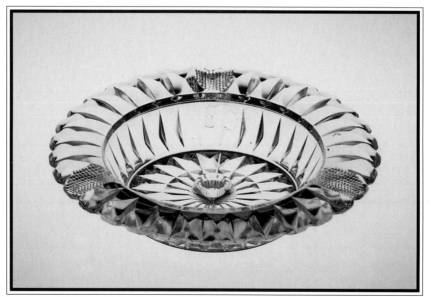

WINDSOR pink ashtray - rare item

Compare this style to the green shown in my 9th edition of the *Collector's Encyclopedia of Depression Glass.*

LANCASTER GLASS COMPANY 1908-1937

Although purchased by Hocking in 1924, Lancaster Glass of Lancaster, Ohio, operated under that name until 1937 when Hocking eliminated the name completely. The plant still operates today as plant #2 of Anchor-Hocking.

JUBILEE yellow 4", 1 oz. cordial - rare item

This is the infamous cordial I received for my April 19th birthday in 1989 some time in May as I was writing my 9th edition of the *Collector's Encyclopedia of Depression Glass*. My wife's memory is eclectic to say the least!

LIBERTY GLASS WORKS 1903-1932

Located in New Jersey instead of the Ohio-Pennsylvania-West Virginia glass-making triangle, this company prospered during the early days of Depression glass until a fire destroyed the plant and it was never rebuilt. They made many utilitarian items and provide us with one of the few dresser sets in pressed wares of the Depression era.

AMERICAN PIONEER pink dresser set - rare item

Although a few of these have been found in green, this is the only one known in pink.

MACBETH-EVANS GLASS COMPANY 1899-1937

Macbeth-Evans made some of the more popular Depression patterns, but as in other companies' wares, some pieces are in such short supply, they're deemed quite rare finds.

AMERICAN SWEETHEART monax with yellow trim cup and saucer - rare color

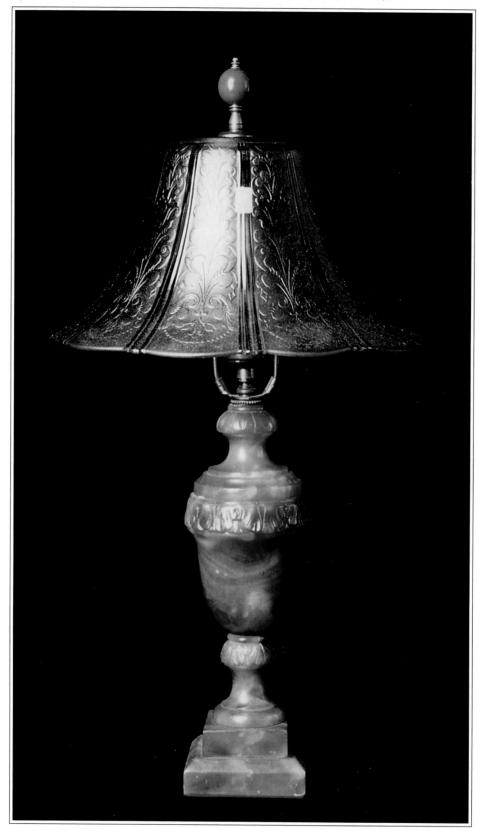

AMERICAN SWEETHEART amber lamp shade - rare color

At one time two of these were found in Canada, but one was broken in shipment, so this is the only one known.

DOGWOOD
mother-of-pearl finish cremax
cake plate - rare color

Author's Collection

Both sides are shown so you can see the pattern that is only on the bottom. I have never seen another piece of this company's glass with this type of finish.

Macbeth-Evans Glass Company

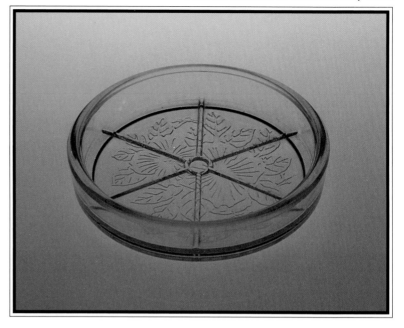

DOGWOOD
pink coaster - rare item

**"S" PATTERN,
"STIPPLED ROSE BAND"**
pink silk screened 80 oz.
pitcher - rare color

McKEE GLASS COMPANY 1853-1951

Originally founded as McKee & Brothers Glass Works at Pittsburgh in Westmoreland County in 1888 and built its new plant there. This site became the town of Jeannette. The move had been necessitated by the availability of natural gas in this area. Later, with the depletion of this natural gas, the company turned to the other readily available resource in the area – coal. McKee continued making glass at this site until 1951 when the Thatcher Glass Company bought the company.

When McKee is mentioned today, two things seem to stand out in collector's minds: Rock Crystal and kitchenware items. Collectors of Depression patterns immediately think of the red or crystal of the Rock Crystal pattern that was made from the early 1900's up until the 1940's. The kitchenware lines of reamers and measuring cups have come to the forefront of collecting in recent years. There were many other kitchenware items made, but these two categories have some of the most avidly sought items.

From the collection of Dan Tucker and Lorrie Kitchen

SAUNDERS black reamer - rare item

I often wondered about the safety of using such a sharply pointed reamer. Now the truth is known! A metallic holder grips the fruit while you turn a knob to "juice" the fruit.

"RADIUM EMANTOR FILTER" canary yellow (vaseline)
water dispenser - rare item

This 21" tall system consists of a 12" bottle which turns up
onto another 12½" bottle and a radium filter was placed
between these to filter the water.

MORGANTOWN GLASS WORKS 1929-1972

First established in Morgantown, West Virginia as Morgantown Glass Works, but became the Economy Glass Tumbler Company in the early 1900's until 1929 when it became Morgantown again. It continued as Morgantown until bought out by Bailey Glass in 1972.

Author's Collection

"DANCING GIRL," (SUNRISE MEDALLION)
blue creamer and sugar - rare item

Thanks to the Old Morgantown Glass Collector's Guild, Inc. for furnishing the actual name of this pattern which collectors have always called "Dancing Girl." No one who collects this pattern seems to be able to find these two pieces.

Author's Collection

NEW MARTINSVILLE GLASS MANUFACTURING COMPANY 1901-1944

The factory became Viking Glass Company in 1944 and is still in operation today. During the Depression era New Martinsville produced quality color control and were known by their Ruby (red) and their Ritz blue (cobalt blue).

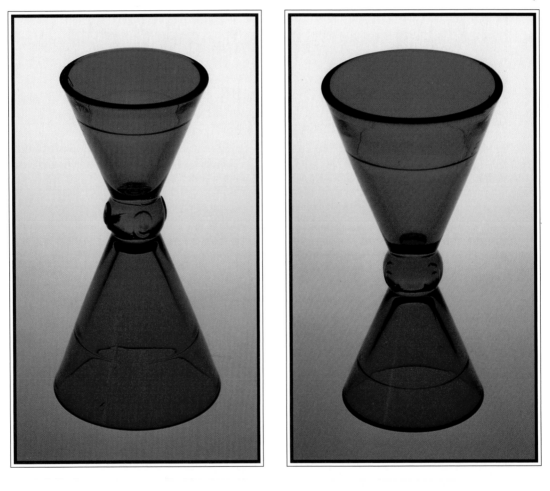

MOONDROPS Ruby double shot glass - rare item

This measures 1 oz. or 2 ozs. depending upon which end you use to measure.

RADIANCE ice blue butter dish - rare item

I found this in Pasadena, California, at a local flea market in March 1990; so there can still be rare items found!

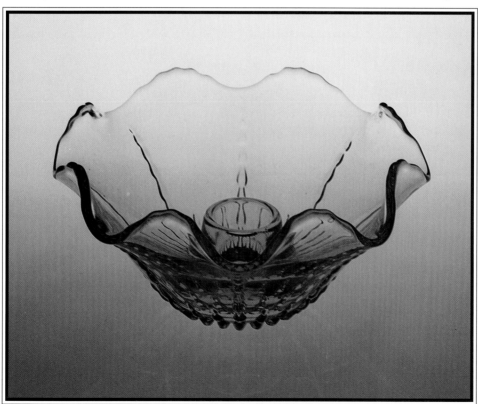

RADIANCE ice blue 6" ruffled candle holder - rare item

From the collection of John and Trannie Davis

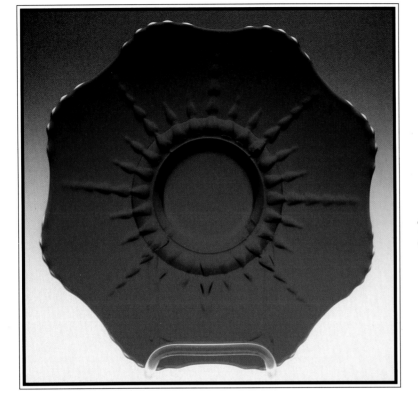

RADIANCE
Ruby miniature cake or candy stand - rare item

This 8" pedestal footed stand is only 2" high.

From the collection of Dennis Bialek

RADIANCE
Ruby 5¼" tall by 6½" wide comport - rare item

PADEN CITY GLASS COMPANY 1916-1951

Paden City Glass Company built its factory and started producing glassware all within a one-year time period. That was considered quite a feat in 1916. We think of Paden City as a company which produced a multitude of colors and made a variety of patterns containing birds. This handmade glass was not turned out in the large quantities that many of the glass factories of that day produced. Hence, items manufactured by Paden City are even more scarce 50 years later. Most of the glassware made by this company is exceedingly attractive in design and line.

Author's Collection

BLACK FOREST blue ice tub - rare color

This is the only piece of blue Black Forest I have seen.

BLACK FOREST pink 8" 62 oz. pitcher - rare item

BLACK FOREST green tumble-up set - rare item

Pitcher stands 6½" and holds 42 ozs., but it is the tumbler that is impossible to find. The tumbler has a ridge which fits inside the pitcher perfectly and allows the tumbler to rest on the rim of the pitcher.

CUPID aqua samovar - rare item

TIFFIN GLASS COMPANY (one of many branches of U.S. Glass)

The U.S. Glass Company was founded in 1891 as a merger of 18 smaller companies in Ohio, Pennsylvania and West Virginia. The branch known as "R" factory was located at Tiffin, Ohio and was better known as the Tiffin Glass Factory.

Author's Collection

FLANDERS pink handled parfait or Irish coffee - rare item

FLANDERS pink 8" vase, cupped Dahlia - rare item

FUCHSIA crystal shrimp or icer - rare item

UNKNOWN

Above left:
"WHITE KING" soap dispenser - rare item

Above right:
"PEACOCK BLUE" one-handle measure cup -
rare item

Right:
"HAWKES" signed red sugar shaker - rare item

Price Guide

Page 52
Madrid "Golden Glo" lazy susan - **$600.00-650.00**

Page 53
Parrot "Golden Glo" butter dish - **$1,000.00-1,100.00**
Parrot Springtime green round hot plate - **$550.00-600.00**

Page 54
American amethyst beer mug - **$100.00-125.00**

Page 55
American blue candlestick - **$125.00-150.00**

Page 56
American blue Tom & Jerry punch bowl - **$1,750.00-2,000.00**

Page 57
American crystal swung vase - **$400.00-500.00**

Page 58
American crystal soap dish - **$600.00-650.00**

Page 59
Chintz red lamp with gold decoration - **value undetermined**

Page 60
Colony green vase - **$150.00-175.00**

Page 61
June blue blown comport - **$125.00-150.00**
June yellow soup bowl - **$95.00-100.00**

Page 62
Navarre crystal carafe - **$300.00-350.00**

Page 63
Navarre green dinner bell - **value undetermined**

Page 64
Trojan Topaz decanter - **$600.00-750.00**

Page 65
Versailles blue decanter - **$1,250.00-1,500.00**

Page 66
Vesper amber Mah Jongg set - **$75.00-100.00**

Page 67
Vesper amber butter dish - **$600.00-750.00**

Page 68
Colonial Block Ritz Blue creamer - **$75.00-100.00**

Page 69
Florentine No. 2 crystal decorated vase - **$150.00-250.00**

Page 70
Florentine No. 2 pink sherbet - **$60.00-75.00**
Florentine No. 2 pink lemonade tumbler - **$75.00-95.00**

Page 71
Florentine No. 2 fired-on orange cup and saucer - **$30.00-50.00**
Florentine No. 2 fired-on blue cup and saucer - **$30.00-50.00**

Page 72
Fruits green rolled edge bowl - **$125.00-150.00**

Page 73
Royal Lace nut bowls, green - **$150.00-175.00**
　　blue - **$250.00-350.00**
　　pink - **$150.00-175.00**

Page 74
Lariat amber high sherbet - **$600.00-650.00**

Page 75
Lodestar Dawn candlestick - **$300.00-400.00**

Page 76
Octagon Hawthorne with Moongleam handles creamer and
　　sugar - **$400.00-450.00 set**

Page 77
Orchid crystal Waverly lemon dish - **$750.00-800.00**

Page 78
Orchid crystal vase - **$600.00-750.00**

Page 79
Plantation crystal cigarette box - **$200.00-250.00**

Page 80
Plantation crystal epergne candle holder - **$100.00-125.00**

Page 81
Provencial zircon vase - **$400.00-500.00**

Page 82
Saturn zircon 2-lite candlestick - **$500.00-600.00**

Page 83
Cobalt blue Old Williamsburg pilsner - **$200.00-250.00**

Page 84
Tangerine Empress cup and saucer - **$650.00-750.00 set**
Tangerine Empress creamer - **$500.00-550.00**
Tangerine Empress sugar - **$500.00-550.00**

Page 85
Empress crystal Maxfield Parrish plate - **$450.00-500.00**

Page 86
Cameo crystal shaker - **$150.00-200.00**

Page 87
Cameo green wine goblet - **$500.00-550.00**

Page 88
Fire-King "Philbe" blue water goblet - **$125.00-150.00**

Page 89
Fire-King "Philbe" blue candy jar - **$850.00-1,000.00**

Page 90
Fire-King "Philbe" green cookie jar - **$700.00-800.00**

Page 91
Mayfair green pitcher - **$400.00-500.00**

Page 92
Mayfair pink cocktail - **$750.00-850.00**

Page 93
Mayfair pink vase - **$5,000.00+**

Page 94
Mayfair pink miniature berry bowl - **value undetermined**
Mayfair yellow octagonal bowl - **$650.00-750.00**

Page 95
Miss America Jade-ite salad plate - **$75.00-85.00**

Page 96
Princess green footed pitcher - **$500.00-600.00**
　　tumbler - **$55.00-75.00**

Schroeder's Antiques Price Guide

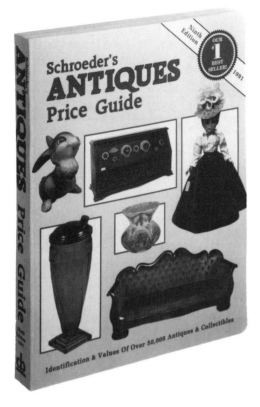

Schroeder's Antiques Price Guide has become THE household name in the antiques & collectibles industry. Our team of editors work year around with more than 200 contributors to bring you our #1 best-selling book on antiques & collectibles.

With more than 50,000 items identified & priced, *Schroeder's* is a must for the collector & dealer alike. If it merits the interest of today's collector, you'll find it in *Schroeder's.* Each subject is represented with histories and background information. In addition, hundreds of sharp original photos are used each year to illustrate not only the rare and unusual, but the everyday "fun-type" collectibles as well -- not postage stamp pictures, but large close-up shots that show important details clearly.

Our editors compile a new book each year. Never do we merely change prices. Accuracy is our primary aim. Prices are gathered over the entire year previous to publication, from ads and personal contacts. Then each category is thoroughly checked to spot inconsistencies, listings that may not be entirely reflective of actual market dealings, and lines too vague to be of merit. Only the best of the lot remains for publication. You'll find *Schroeder's Antiques Price Guide* the one to buy for factual information and quality.

No dealer, collector or investor can afford not to own this book. It is available from your favorite bookseller or antiques dealer at the low price of $12.95. If you are unable to find this price guide in your area, it's available from Collector Books, P.O. Box 3009, Paducah, KY 42002-3009 at $12.95 plus $2.00 for postage and handling.

8½ x 11", 608 Pages   **$12.95**

COLLECTOR BOOKS
A Division of Schroeder Publishing Co., Inc.